INFORMATION
EXPLORER
JUNIOR

Choose It!
Finding the Right
Research Topic

CHERRY LAKE PUBLISHING • ANN ARBOR, MICHIGAN

CHERRY LAKE Publishing

A NOTE TO PARENTS AND TEACHERS: Please remind your children how to stay safe online before they do the activities in this book.

A NOTE TO KIDS: Always remember your safety comes first!

Published in the United States of America
by Cherry Lake Publishing
Ann Arbor, Michigan
www.cherrylakepublishing.com

Content Adviser: Gail Dickinson, PhD, Professor,
Old Dominion University, Norfolk, Virginia

Photo Credits: Cover, © Eric Cote/Shutterstock.com; page 5, © Monkey Business Images/Shutterstock.com; page 7, © KPG_Payless/Shutterstock.com; page 9, © Robert Kneschke/Shutterstock.com; pages 10 and 14, © Tyler Olson/Shutterstock. com; page 13, © Dmytro Vietrov/Shutterstock.com; page 18, © Olesya Feketa/ Shutterstock.com; page 20, © Richard Paul Kane/Shutterstock.com.

Library of Congress Cataloging-in-Publication Data
Coleman, Kelly, 1976–
  Choose it! : finding the right research topic / by Kelly Coleman.
    pages cm. — (Information explorer junior)
  Includes bibliographical references and index.
  ISBN 978-1-63188-862-5 (lib. bdg.) — ISBN 978-1-63188-874-8 (pbk.) —
ISBN 978-1-63188-886-1 (pdf) —ISBN 978-1-63188-898-4 (e-book)
  1. Research—Methodology—Juvenile literature. 2. Report writing—
Juvenile literature. I. Title.

  ZA3080.C64 2015
  001.4'2—dc23   2014024986

Cherry Lake Publishing would like to acknowledge the work of The Partnership for 21st Century Skills. Please visit www.p21.org for more information.

Printed in the United States of America
Corporate Graphics Inc.
January 2015

Table of Contents

CHAPTER ONE

What Is Research?

Have you ever wondered, "Why is the sky blue?" Maybe you have watched a cartoon and asked, "Why do cats chase mice?" Or perhaps you have noticed trash on the side of the road. Did you think, "Where does this trash come from?" If you have ever asked a question and then worked to find the answer, you have done

Even cartoons can lead to research questions.

Ms. Patel's students have a lot of ideas for their projects.

research. Research is a process to answer questions about a certain topic.

A research topic is the subject a person wants to learn about. For example, Ms. Patel asks her students to research questions about fish for a class project. There is a lot of information to learn about fish. Entire books have been written about them! Ms. Patel's students have to narrow this general topic down to a more specific topic for their projects. This topic should be turned into a question.

There are many things you could learn about fish.

Each student thinks about what he or she most wants to learn about fish. To help them, Ms. Patel asks, "What would you ask an expert about fish?"

Susie asks, "Why do humans need fish?"

Jack wonders, "What is the best way to catch a fish in Lake Michigan?"

Martina wants to know, "Why are fish in oceans different from fish in lakes?"

Once the students have each chosen a topic and written a question, they can begin their research. They find **resources**. They read and take notes. In the end, they combine everything they learned into a paper, presentation, or other project. Research is exciting. But there are so many interesting topics to wonder about. In this book, you will learn some **strategies** to help you choose a research topic.

Books are one type of resource you might use in a research project.

To get a copy of this activity, visit
www.cherrylakepublishing.com/activities.

Try This

Let's practice forming questions about different topics. Copy the chart below onto a separate sheet of paper. Leave some spaces between each topic. Under "Questions," list some questions you might ask about each topic.

Topic	Questions
Soccer	
China	
Water pollution	
Abraham Lincoln	

STOP!
Don't write in the book!

CHAPTER TWO

Choosing a Topic

Some teachers might have a few guidelines to share with the class.

Before you choose a research topic and question, you need to know about any **guidelines** you should follow. A guideline is like a rule. Is the research part of a school project? If so, your teacher may give some

Mr. Stone's guidelines make it easy for him to help his students find resources.

guidelines about choosing and researching your topic. For example, Mr. Stone gives his students only a few topics to choose from. Mrs. Nelson assigns each of her students a research topic. Mr. Welstein and Ms. Anton give their students a list of facts to find or questions to answer about their topics. Mr. Alvez lets his students choose what they will learn.

As another example, Ari decides to do research because a topic interests him. He is curious about a topic and excited to learn more about it. The research is not part of a class project. There are not any guidelines from a teacher he has to follow. He gets to decide what is important and which questions to answer.

Once you have a general topic, you need to come up with a specific research question. You may want to start by **brainstorming** a list of questions. Brainstorming is writing things down as soon as they pop into your mind. You do not stop to worry about spelling. You do not edit your list as you go. This way, you keep your creativity flowing. When you brainstorm, you may find that the ideas that pop up first are topics that are important to you.

Work quickly to get the best brainstorming results.

To get a copy of this activity, visit www.cherrylakepublishing.com/activities.

Try This

Set a timer for 5 minutes. Grab a notebook and pencil. A computer or tablet will also work. Write your research topic at the top of your page. Then start the timer. Use the 5 minutes to brainstorm questions about your topic. See how many questions you can add to your list in that time. Remember, do not edit your questions while the timer is ticking! You will have plenty of time later to check your list and figure out which questions are best.

Keep going until the timer runs down!

CHAPTER THREE

Narrowing Down Your Topic

You should have several good ideas to choose from by now.

Now that you have some ideas about what interests you, it's time to narrow down your list. When you do this, you decide which question is the best or most important. This can be a challenge. So where do you start?

Some kinds of information might be found only in books.

Rachel has a list of questions to choose from for a school presentation. To narrow down the list, she first simply crosses off any questions she does not find interesting. After all, it's no fun to research something you're not a little curious about!

Next, Rachel thinks about what resources she would need to research the remaining questions. Are resources available online?

She and her grandfather perform an Internet search for each question. They look for kid-friendly sites that will help Rachel find answers. Rachel also checks the library. She asks a librarian what materials are available for her questions. Do they have enough information? The information also needs to be written in a way she can understand.

Searching online is a great way to find information quickly.

Finally, Rachel thinks about the **purpose** of her research. A purpose is the reason a person does something. Knowing her purpose helps Rachel decide which question is best. Depending on what the purpose is, different strategies might be more helpful than others. A few possible strategies are listed in the chart below.

Purpose for Research	Strategies for Narrowing Topic
To show to a teacher what you've learned.	• Show your list to a classmate. What does he or she think is best? • Share your list with your teacher. Discuss which questions best fit any guidelines for the assignment.
To share information with friends who have similar interests.	• Think about which of the topics or questions you love the most. Which questions get you the most excited? Which have you been wondering about the longest?

To get a copy of this activity, visit www.cherrylakepublishing.com/activities.

Try This

At the top of a separate piece of paper, write, "The purpose of my research is _____." Then list any strategies from the chart on page 16 that might help you narrow down your research topic. Try each strategy you listed. Put a star next to the one that helped you most. Now write down which research topic you have chosen in your notebook. Why did you choose that topic?

Revising Your Question

Chapter Four:
Revising Your Question

Adjust your question until you get it just right.

Now you have a topic and a question to research. Next, you need to make sure you have asked the question in just the right way. You might be thinking, "What?!

There is a *wrong* way to ask a question?" There may not be a wrong way, but there are ways to ask a question that will help you find better information. For example, Carlos asks, "What is the most popular sport in America?" Carlos loves sports. This question interests him very much. However, when Carlos researches this question, he only finds a one-word answer. That does not give him much to write about in his research project. This is what is called a **closed question**. Closed questions give short answers or can be answered with a "yes" or "no."

Closed questions are not very good for research projects.

There are many open questions you could ask about baseball.

When researching, it is best to ask **open questions**. Open questions help you find more detailed information. They can help you find out why something is true. Carlos learns that baseball is the most popular sport in America. How can he ask an open question about his topic? He could ask, "How is baseball different from other sports?" Or he could ask, "How has baseball changed over time?"

Once you have a good, open question that you like, it is time to get to work. You are well on your way to a great research project!

To get a copy of this activity, visit www.cherrylakepublishing.com/activities.

Try This

The chart below has examples of closed questions. Work with a classmate to turn these topics into open questions. Then look at your own research question. Is it closed or open? How can you revise it to find the best possible information?

Closed Questions	Open Questions
Who was the first president of the United States?	
How deep is the ocean?	
Where do lions live?	
What started the Civil War?	

STOP!
Don't write in the book!

Glossary

brainstorming **(BRAYN-storm-ing)** coming up with ideas or solutions to a problem

closed question **(KLOWZD KWES-chuhn)** a question that can be answered with "yes," "no," or another simple piece of information

guidelines **(GIDE-linez)** general rules

open questions **(OH-pin KWES-chuhnz)** questions that require more than a simple answer

purpose **(PUR-puhs)** a goal or an aim

resources **(REE-sors-iz)** something that provides information or that a person can go to for help or support

strategies **(STRAT-i-jeez)** clever plans for achieving a goal

22

Find Out More

BOOKS

Gaines, Ann Graham. *Ace Your Research Paper*. Berkeley Heights, NJ: Enslow Publishers, 2009.

Green, Julie. *Write It Down*. Ann Arbor, MI: Cherry Lake Publishing, 2010.

Harner, Jennifer L. *Reading and Learning from Informational Text*. Ann Arbor, MI: Cherry Lake Publishing, 2014.

WEB SITES

American Association of School Librarians— KidsConnect's Research Toolbox
www.ala.org/aasl/standards-guidelines/kidsconnect
Learn more tips on how to ask the best kind of question, as well as how to start researching, understanding, and sharing what you learn.

Kentucky Virtual Library Presents: How to Do Research
www.kyvl.org/kids/f_homebase.html
Find a ton of information on how to produce a first-rate research project.

Index

About the Author

Kelly Coleman is a school library media specialist in Illinois. She enjoys reading, creative writing, and playing with her dogs, Harry and Neville.